Th

Morale Crisis

Break the Cycle

JOSHUA S. CHASE

DISCLAIMER

The recommendations, thoughts, descriptions, advice, and methods in this book are solely for educational purposes. The author assumes no liability whatsoever for any loss or damage that results from the use of any of the material in this book.

Published By: The Chase Collective LLC

Cover Design: Joshua S. Chase

Edited By: Joe Pierson

ISBN: 9798342485579

DEDICATION

To all the men and women in the fire service who have stopped complaining about our morale problems and have started to do something about them. Keep bringing solutions to the problems.

CONTENTS

FOREWORD

I was happy to have Josh ask me to write the foreword for his book. Morale, as he mentions, is something that can ebb and flow from day to day. He will get into some of the things that contribute to high morale, as well as things that can destroy it. What this really came down to for me when I read the book was ownership. Morale starts with *you*! Should your captains, chiefs, and fire chief care? Of course, they should, but often, one sole person can't take the blame for a morale problem. There is a quote from a US Army general that I have always liked and is used primarily to address leaders in a formal capacity. I go back to this quote when I find myself asking, *Am I in control? Am I doing everything I am supposed to before I point the finger at someone else?* The quote from General Bruce Clark goes like this: "When things go wrong under your command, start wading for the reason in increasingly larger concentric circles around your desk."

What the general was getting at here is taking ownership and having some self-reflection. While you may not be in a formal leadership position, you can have the same mindset the general has. You can ask yourself something every day, because we have a choice, right? We can ask ourselves, *When I walk into the firehouse, am I going to use my attitude and actions to improve morale, or am I going to contribute to its erosion?* This is a decision that must be made regardless of what is happening outside those four walls. Now, are there real problems that exist in our organizations? At times there are, but I go back to the fact—not opinion, fact—that firefighters and company officers have the ability to skyrocket morale when conditions outside your firehouse would say no way possible. How do I know? Because I have seen it!

Sometimes it's very easy to point the finger up the chain of command or seek to blame others. It's harder to be reflective and put ourselves in front of a mirror and ask, *Am I in direct control of the conditions I create when I come to work?* Are your higher-ups sometimes to blame? Sure, they are, but sometimes the blame lies a little further down the organizational chart. In the end, we are all responsible and should ask ourselves that question. From the brand-new firefighter to the fire chief. Every single one of us contributes collectively to high or low morale. Firefighting is a team sport, and we don't get the option to sit the bench on morale!

Josh is going to give you practical and realistic ways to improve morale in your firehouse. Is he going to give you the silver bullet to solve all your organizational issues? Probably not. What I can tell you is that you are going to hear from someone who practices what he preaches. Josh is a company officer and gives meaning to the words on these pages every shift. He takes morale in his firehouse seriously and demonstrates ownership. The advice in this book is genuine. In the title you read, *The Fire Service Morale Crisis*. As you read this, you may be in one right now. If so, I hope you are able to pull some valuable information to help you skyrocket morale in your firehouses and contribute to the overall health of your organizations. You may be reading this and be in a situation where morale is through the roof. That's awesome! Use this book as a guide and a road map to help others who may not be in your situation. I wish all of you the best! Take action and take ownership, because if not *you*, then who?

Jarrod Sergi

Fire Battalion Chief

INTRODUCTION

Morale in the fire service is more than just a buzzword; it is the foundation upon which effective operations, teamwork, and the overall well-being of our firefighters is built. Unfortunately, it seems like an uninterrupted culture cycle of negativity is stopping us from enjoying our careers. Some would say that we are in the middle of a morale crisis. If that's the case, it's time to break the cycle, my friends.

A myriad of problems affect the fire service, good and bad. Recognizing that this impacts morale is key to making sure you and those around you are able to not only succeed in your career, but also enjoy it. High morale fuels motivation, fosters a positive work environment, and strengthens the bonds among fire crews. Conversely, low morale can lead to disengagement, increased stress, diminished performance, recruitment problems, and retainment issues, all of which can impact not only the safety of our communities and efficiency of operations but also the family life, mental health, and job satisfaction of firefighters.

I'm writing this book to not only address the complex and multifaceted nature of morale in the fire service, but to offer you practical steps and a perspective that will help you enjoy your career. It's my goal to provide more of a comprehensive look at what constitutes morale, why it matters, and how it can be both positively and negatively influenced. Based on my personal experiences, of course.

As you read through the pages, you'll notice it reads more like a reference manual. I want you to be able to pick this book up at any time for some quick advice and encouragement. It is a book you can hand to someone who is struggling with some of these issues and give them a new perspective. A road map back to sanity when you get off track.

Similar to the other books I have written, I'll share from experiences and hope that you relate. It's worked so far. After all, if you're reading this, it's probably because you care. After almost twenty years in the fire service, I've had my moments! I've had my moments with leadership, communication, and team building—just a few of the things we'll get into. I've had some pretty significant morale challenges with work-life balance too. Significant enough to almost take me out of the fire service for good. We'll get into that.

This book offers practical advice and real-world examples to guide fire service leaders (you) and your crew in fostering a supportive and motivating environment. We will define morale and learn to understand its significance within the fire service. We're going to highlight how a positive or negative morale can shape the experiences of firefighters, the community, and their families.

We're not going to just talk about morale, we're going to address practical ways to improve morale, effective leadership strategies, the importance of communication, and the impact of recognition and team-building activities. I have some good ones you can do right in your station. Additionally, I'll address common pitfalls that can harm morale, such as poor leadership and the classic burnout and provide guidance on how to counteract these challenges.

The Fire Service Morale Crisis: Breaking the Cycle is more than just a quick reference manual for addressing morale issues; it is a call to action. For fire service leaders, supervisors, and fire crews to prioritize and cultivate a healthy, positive work environment, while still maintaining the standard of service we took an oath to fulfill. By breaking the cycle of low morale and implementing the strategies outlined in this book, I aim to build a stronger, more resilient fire service that is better equipped to handle the demands of our critical roles. Let's go.

SECTION 1:

UNDERSTANDING MORALE IN THE FIRE SERVICE

Defining Morale

Technically speaking, according to Google, morale is a psychological state that reflects the level of enthusiasm, confidence, and satisfaction an individual or group has within a workplace or organization. In this case, the fire service. Simply put, it's in your brain, bro. It's in your brain, and you will make decisions that come from your feelings that will impact how you see morale. It encompasses the collective attitudes, emotions, and overall energy of your fire crew. Good or bad, it exists.

High or good morale typically signifies that your crew is motivated, engaged, and committed to their work. Low morale is the complete opposite. Low morale indicates dissatisfaction, disengagement, and a lack of motivation. Big surprise, right? In any organization, particularly the fire service, morale plays a crucial role in shaping the performance, effectiveness, and overall well-being of its members and directly impacts the community. Often when it comes to morale in the fire service, the community is not discussed. Which is strange to me, seeing as how they are direct recipients of the culture we foster in our stations and departments. High morale, high customer service. Low morale, low customer service. It's not rocket science. It's firefighter science. It's simple.

It is important to remember that morale is more than just a feel-good factor; it is the key component of operational success. High morale within a fire crew leads to better communication, stronger teamwork, and a greater sense of camaraderie—that word a lot of us say doesn't exist anymore. Firefighters with high morale are more likely to trust their colleagues, follow their leaders, follow their coworkers, and maintain a positive outlook, even in the face of adversity. This is key, considering that adversity is our job. It's the career that we chose.

The Impact of Positive Morale

Everyone wants to go to work and be happy. I like going to work knowing I'm going to have a good day. No one wants to go to the firehouse and enjoy a shitty day of work where morale is low and everything sucks. It's draining, and the men and women contributing to low morale are draining to be around. So, what are the impacts of positive morale in the fire service? That's what the rest of this chapter is about, and some of us seriously need to embrace this.

Enhanced Teamwork and Cohesion

Morale directly impacts the ability of a fire service crew to work together effectively. In high-pressure situations, such as battling the dragon (also known as fire) or executing a rescue operation, seamless teamwork is essential. High morale fosters a sense of unity and shared purpose, encouraging your fire crew to support each other, communicate openly, and collaborate effectively. When morale is high, firefighters are more likely to step up, cover for one another, hug each other's back, and work as a cohesive unit, which is vital for the safety and success of any operation. With increased teamwork and unit cohesion, things like gossip and getting in trouble for stupid things tends to cease. It's a natural byproduct.

Improved Performance and Efficiency

Firefighters with high morale are more likely to be engaged and motivated in their station and operational duties. This engagement leads to better performance, as individuals are more willing to go above and beyond in their roles. High morale also contributes to a proactive approach to problem-solving, where firefighters are more inclined to take initiative, make quick decisions, and adapt to changing circumstances. This creates a culture of ownership that is followed directly by the culture of informal leadership. Which I am a huge fan of, if you didn't know already.

Increased Resilience in High-Stress Situations

The nature of firefighting and emergency medical services is inherently stressful. We often face dangerous and unpredictable situations and scenarios. High morale helps build resilience, enabling firefighters to cope with stress more effectively. What is resilience? It's the capacity to withstand or to recover quickly from difficulties. When morale is high, individuals are better equipped to handle the emotional and psychological toll of their work, reducing the likelihood of burnout, anxiety, and other stress-related issues. This resilience not only benefits the individual firefighter but also ensures that the crew remains strong and capable, even under the most challenging conditions.

Positive Impact on Mental Health and Well-Being

Morale is closely linked to the mental health and well-being of firefighters. High morale can contribute to a positive work environment, where individuals feel valued, supported, and respected. This positive environment can mitigate the effects of the traumatic experiences that firefighters often encounter, helping them maintain their mental health and well-being. On the other hand, low morale can exacerbate feelings of isolation, stress, and depression, leading to a decline in mental health and, in some cases, contributing to issues such as substance abuse or PTSD. For the sake of staying on topic, I'm going to leave this one here, but I encourage you to take a personal look into where you are right now. How is morale affecting your own mental health? It may be time for you to seek some help or talk to someone. I have sought counseling for my mental health on more than one occasion and it has been more than helpful for me.

Retention and Recruitment

Morale also plays a significant role in the retention and recruitment of firefighters. High morale can create a positive reputation for a fire department, making it an attractive place to work. This reputation can help in recruiting new members who are eager to join a department with a strong sense of camaraderie and purpose. Conversely, low morale can lead to high turnover rates, as dissatisfied firefighters may seek opportunities elsewhere. A situation that's going on all over the fire service right now. We're out here robbing each other and paying our debts with the bounty. The loss of experienced firefighters can be costly, both financially and in terms of operational effectiveness, as it takes time to train and integrate new recruits. Honestly, my department is experiencing some of this right now. We have also recognized it, acknowledged it, and are actively taking steps to address it. The first step is acknowledgment. For your department to fix a problem, it has to acknowledge it first.

When it comes to the positive impact of morale, there are probably a few others that I left out, but these are the ones I saw as a priority. The ones I feel like we deal with on a daily basis. In the fire service, morale is not just a matter of personal satisfaction; this is not a fairy tale where you just get what you want and feel good all the time. It is a vital component that influences every aspect of your work as a firefighter or an officer.

Before we move on, I will say this for leaders. Leaders within the fire service must recognize the importance of morale and take proactive steps to nurture and maintain it, ensuring that their crews are prepared to face the challenges of their profession with confidence, unity, and determination. Fire service leaders directly impact the morale of the fire service. This must be recognized and acknowledged. If you've read any of my other fire service books, you know what I mean when I say *leaders*. I'm not only talking about the men and women with bugles or trumpets. When I address leaders, I am not talking about specifically officers; I am talking about any member at any rank who has any amount of influence to positively impact morale. You can grab *Jump Seat Leadership* if you're curious about what leadership looks like without a title.

SECTION 2:

POSITIVE IMPACT ON FIREHOUSE MORALE

If you noticed, I did not name this chapter "Positive Fire Service Morale" or "Positive Fire Department Morale." I believe changing the big fire service starts with changing the small fire service. Your firehouse. You have to make sure morale is good where you go to work every day. You may not be able to fix your department, but you can influence the men and women you work with on a daily basis.

Leadership

Effective leadership is the cornerstone of high morale in the fire service. Leaders set the tone for the entire crew, and their actions directly influence the attitudes and behaviors of their members. A good leader fosters an environment of trust, respect, and support, which are essential for maintaining high morale. A shitty leader obviously does the opposite.

Leaders can improve morale by being approachable and genuinely caring about the well-being of their team. This includes being present and engaged, listening to concerns, and taking action to address issues promptly. By demonstrating empathy (a word the fire service is still learning to understand), leaders show that they value their firefighters as individuals, not just as employees. This sense of being valued can significantly boost morale. Simply put, treat your people like people. Not fire service employee robots that were cloned in a lab to complete an operational task.

Don't forget, leaders should be leading by example, displaying the qualities they wish to see in their crew, such as dedication, professionalism, engagement, and a positive attitude. When firefighters see their officers and leaders embodying these traits, they are more likely to mirror them, creating a positive and motivated team dynamic. It all hinges on leadership. You find a place with poor morale, you can most likely look to the leader to see what's going on, and I'm not talking about the "titled" leader. Some of you know what I'm talking about.

As a captain in the fire service, I understand that I directly impact the well-being of my team. I consider myself solely responsible for the state of morale in my firehouse. Am I responsible for everyone's feelings and reactions? Nope. I am, however, responsible for fostering a culture where my crew wants to come to work every day. Do I get it right all the time? Nope. How do I know when I get it wrong? I ask my crew. I've given them a voice. My team has input in how I run the station and how they want to be treated. Does that compromise standards? Nope. I've found that when my crew at the firehouse feels they have a voice, they meet standards without question.

My strategy? Every month we have a "family meeting." We talk about station life, home life, work-life balance, etc. It's a morale checkup, if you will. We have an open and honest conversation with each other. My crew has a voice, and I suggest you give your crew a voice too. Do I like everything they say? Nope. But it's important that I know what's going on within my crew, versus not giving them a voice and them talking behind my back. Because that's exactly what will happen. I did this as a firefighter too. We had monthly meetings with the crew, and the senior firefighter would bring concerns to the officer. It works at both levels.

Now, with all that said, you will run into the person who wants nothing to do what I just wrote, and you might work for or be this person. If you work for this person and there is no possibility of change, you might want to look at a transfer or wait the person out. If you are this person and you know it, start giving your crew a voice and take their input and feedback when it comes to morale in their firehouse. Leadership and morale go hand in hand.

Communication

It's no surprise that the next thing here is communication. Clear, consistent, and open communication is vital to improving morale in the fire service. It's important that this is effective. Sometimes we are talking, but we are not communicating. When communication channels are open and effective, crews feel informed, included, and connected to the larger mission. I cannot stress this enough. This sense of inclusion fosters a sense of belonging and purpose. Once again, it also significantly cuts down on gossip and rumors.

To enhance communication, leaders should prioritize transparency, keeping team members informed about decisions, changes, and the reasons behind them. This reduces uncertainty and builds trust at the station level, when firefighters feel they are part of the decision-making process and are not left in the dark. I understand we have a chain of command and there are things we can't share all the time. However, we are not the CIA, and there is no top-secret information floating around in the fire service.

Regular, two-way communication is also important. Leaders should create opportunities for the firefighters to voice their opinions, concerns, and suggestions. This can be done through regular meetings (like the one I mentioned) or informal check-ins. You don't always have to have a meeting. Sometimes it's a cup of coffee and a couch. When firefighters feel heard and see their feedback being acted upon, it reinforces their sense of value and respect. It doesn't make sense to me, the number of officers we have in the fire service who are the only "voice" in their stations. They silence their crew with an "I know it all" mentality and then wonder why everyone is so quiet. Just a little help for you here. We function as a team. Every team has a leader, but we still function as a team. Each team member has strengths that can contribute to the overall success of the mission. Once again, not rocket science. That's why I joined the fire service. It's actually pretty simple.

Recognition

Recognition is one of the most powerful tools for boosting morale. We say we don't want to be recognized, but it's okay to be recognized. This "tough as shit" culture we've had in the past has backfired on us in a couple of areas, recognition being one of them. When firefighters feel their hard work and dedication are acknowledged and appreciated, it reinforces their sense of purpose and motivates them to continue performing at their best.

There are so many ways to recognize your crews. From formal awards and commendations to simple verbal praise. You know, use words like "thank you." What matters most is that recognition is sincere, timely, and specific. Recognizing individual and team achievements, especially in front of the crew, can have a profound impact on morale. It not only makes the recipient feel valued but also encourages others to strive for similar recognition. Nothing wrong with a little healthy competition in the fire service.

In addition to individual recognition, celebrating the crew's successes is equally important. Acknowledging the collective efforts of the crew, especially after a challenging fire or call, fosters a sense of pride and camaraderie. These shared moments of recognition help build a strong crew identity and boost overall morale.

We must stop waiting for the executive staff to come down and recognize the men and women we work with every day. As leaders in the fire service and in the stations, it's on us. It's on everyone. Not just a few. There are some departments out there that are crushing this right now. If you're not one of them, there is always room to get better. If you need some ideas, reach out, I got you.

Team building

Admittedly, this one might be one of my favorite things besides the leadership part in this chapter. Team building is essential for fostering strong relationships, trust, crew identity, and unity within the fire service, all of which contribute to high morale.

When firefighters feel connected to their crew, they are more likely to work together effectively, support each other, and maintain a positive outlook, even in the most challenging of situations. I feel like I'm hitting on some things you already know here but may not be practicing.

Team building activities can take many forms, from formal training exercises to informal social gatherings. I enjoy some formal training exercises with my crew that relate functionally to the job we do. Training exercises that require collaboration and problem-solving not only improve operational skills but also strengthen the bonds between crew members. These shared experiences help build trust and mutual respect, which are crucial for effective teamwork and high morale. In short, these team building exercises simulate going to fires on a regular basis, which most of us are not doing now. Think about that feeling you get after you and your crew just got a good stop at a fire. There is no better morale builder than a house fire. Fortunately for homeowners, they are not happening every day.

Unfortunately for us, we now have to create effective ways to build and foster our firefighters.

Informal team building activities, such as group outings, station meals, or recreational events, provide opportunities for your crew to connect on a personal level. Believe it or not, these interactions will break down barriers, foster friendships, and create a supportive team environment. When firefighters feel that they are part of a close-knit group, they are more likely to feel motivated, engaged, and committed to their work. When they don't, they tend to isolate, keep to themselves, and treat work like work. You will not hear from them at all on their days off, and they probably will not reach out if they need help. Start building a team within your firehouse. Just because you have a roster doesn't mean you have a team, and it certainly doesn't mean you have a family.

This takes intentional effort on the leader's part. Something as small as having brunch on a weekend shift can spark some team building and conversation. At my station, every weekend we are on shift, we work out first thing in the morning and make breakfast as a crew. If we are on shift on a Sunday, as the station officer, I make breakfast for the crew. Guys, it's breakfast. It gets people around the table and talking.

Before we move on, I feel like I should mention one thing. The biggest hindrance to building a healthy crew in the fire station is station cliques. Disband that shit immediately. There is a difference between a few guys who get along really well and a station clique. Cliques intentionally look to exclude others with a "we're better than them" mentality. They have no place in the fire service, and nothing will destroy your effort to build a cohesive unit quicker. Honestly, this clique could exist because there was no team. So, they created a team within the team. If that's the case, call it out; it's time to get everyone on the same page.

Work-Life Balance

Work-life balance is a critical factor in maintaining high morale in the fire service. I can't say enough about this one. Especially since I completely mishandled this one after my years in the army and early on in my fire service career. I was almost divorced firefighter and a single dad of three kids. I had *no* balance and let the job take a toll on me. I actually wrote an entire book about that season and how to navigate through some of these challenges. It's called *Engage the Enemy: Fight for Your Purpose*. So, I'm not going to spend a whole lot of time on this one. I highly encourage you to read that book if you are struggling with work-life balance and it's affecting your morale.

With that said, the demanding nature of firefighting— with its long shifts, unpredictable hours, holidays worked, birthdays missed, and exposure to repeated traumatic events—can take a toll on us both physically and mentally. Ensuring that your firefighters have the opportunity to balance their professional responsibilities with personal life is essential for sustaining morale and overall well-being. Please don't take this section being short as a matter of me not seeing it as important. Grab *Engage the Enemy: Fight for Your Purpose* and read it if you genuinely need more information on work-life balance. It's a short, easy read, and I bet you can get it where you got this book.

The Importance of Downtime

It's no secret that we work extended hours under stressful conditions, which can easily lead to burnout if not managed properly. Providing sufficient downtime on shift and between shifts is crucial for allowing firefighters to rest, recharge, and also spend quality time with their families and loved ones when not at work. When firefighters are well rested, they are more likely to be focused, alert, and motivated during their shifts, leading to better performance and higher morale. Exhausted people make decisions from a place of exhaustion and tend to cut corners.

Speaking from experience here. Does anyone make great decisions when they're tired?

I know we are in a nationwide staffing crisis at the time I am writing this book, but encouraging firefighters to take their leave and use vacation time is still an important aspect of promoting work-life balance. Time away from work allows individuals to disconnect from the stresses of the job, engage in hobbies or activities they enjoy, and return to work refreshed, instead of just returning to work. For me, quality family time and jiu jitsu refreshes me. For you it might be fishing, boating, hunting, golf, or just spending quality time with the family. Leaders should not only be actively supporting and promoting the use of leave, but encouraging refreshing activities when your crew is off. Maybe invite one of the crew to take part in your hobby one day.

Now, downtime at work? I am a huge advocate of this. I have worked in a busy city my entire career and have seen this mismanaged and have mismanaged it myself! If I'm brutally honest, I used to think this was the biggest crock of shit when I first joined the fire service. Downtime at work? Downtime is for people who don't want to be here. Right? Wrong. Downtime is for the ones you want to still be here doing the job in thirty years! Downtime keeps people coming to work. Especially in the schedule that I work in. Keep in mind, you may have an "easy" schedule according to some, but downtime is important.

There is nothing wrong with taking time for yourself while you are on shift and enjoying some downtime between calls. I agree that training needs to happen, and the day's tasks need to get done, but not at the cost of your crew coming to work exhausted and dreading coming to work every single day. If there is nothing to do that day other than run calls, let your crew "have the day." We all know we have to get on the truck when the brass hits. Don't create unnecessary busy work for the crew for the sake of "working while you're at work." I hate busy work. As a captain, I don't assign tasks to just keep people busy. It's stupid. I don't like being given work just to stay busy, so I don't do it.

I know there are things we have to get done every day, calls we have to go on, and standards that we have to meet. We are 100 percent going to do those things. Just make sure you keep an eye on your crew if they seem exhausted and allow them the downtime at work if you can recover. Hell, I'm not going to lie; sometimes I create "Fridays." I'll see that my crew has been taking a beating in or outside of work and tell them, "Well, today is Friday (even if it's Monday), so take it easy and just make sure you're on the truck when the brass hits." I usually see a sigh of relief, and it's appreciated. I don't do that every day, but I definitely do.

It usually ends up with us relaxing and enjoying some downtime together. Once the pressure of the day's tasks is gone, the mood is always a little lighter, and people start opening up. This has led to so many good conversations as we were just sitting on the bumper of the rig. Next thing you know, there's coffee cups and cigars out. Remember the team building we talked about earlier? Sometimes your crew just needs a "day off" at work. Warning, though. Too many of these unchecked can lead to a lazy crew. I've seen this go both ways. Balance here is key.

Mental Health and Well-Being Programs

The mental health aspect of firefighter life cannot be overstated. These days I feel like this goes without saying. Regular exposure to traumatic events can lead to conditions such as PTSD, anxiety, substance-abuse issues, and depression. Unfortunately, I have been there and am still learning how to manage some of it. Now, I don't so much abuse my whiskey as much as responsibly enjoy it. Your department should prioritize mental health by offering programs and resources that help firefighters cope with the psychological demands of the job.

Access to counseling, peer support groups, and stress-management workshops are valuable resources that can help us maintain a healthy work-life balance. Leaders should know how to access these resources, encourage the use of them, and actively work to destigmatize mental health issues within the fire station and fire service as a whole. When firefighters feel that their mental health is supported, they are more likely to maintain a positive outlook and higher morale, even in the face of adversity.

If your department does not have its own program, there are many nationwide programs that are out there and willing to help. Next Rung is one of them. They offer free resources to first responders and can be reached at *nextrung.org*. I have sought mental health help on more than one occasion throughout my career, and I am glad I did. We are slowly coming to a place where it's no longer popular to overlook mental health. The "suck it up, buttercup" days are further and further behind us. Thank God. From where I sit, the stigma is slowly dying, and I hope for our sake, the old attitude about mental health never sees the light of day again.

These are just a few things that can have a positive impact on morale in your fire station. They would probably help morale across your department if you passed this information around. Creating a positive morale culture starts with leadership. When leaders demonstrate that it is possible to balance the demands of firefighting with a fulfilling personal life, it sets a positive example for the entire crew.

Additionally, open discussions about the importance of work-life balance should be encouraged within the department. By normalizing conversations about the challenges of balancing work and personal life, leaders can help create an environment where firefighters feel comfortable seeking support when needed. This culture of balance not only improves morale but also contributes to the long-term sustainability of the fire service workforce.

By providing sufficient downtime, supporting mental health, and fostering a culture that values personal well-being, you can help your crews achieve a healthy balance between their professional and personal lives. This balance not only enhances individual well-being but also leads to more motivated, engaged, and resilient crews, ultimately benefiting fire service morale as a whole.

SECTION 3:

WHY RELATIONSHIPS ARE IMPORTANT IN THE FIRE SERVICE

Trust

Why are relationships in the fire service important? One simple word: trust. Trust is the foundation of an effective crew. Trust among crewmembers ensures that everyone feels confident in each other's abilities and judgments, which is essential for smooth operations during emergencies. Have you ever worked with men and women you don't trust? Do I need research here to tell you that it sucks and it's super awkward? I don't think I do. It's not fun to look over at that jump seat next to yours and see someone you don't trust. That person eventually becomes hard to like.

In the fire service, trust is built over time through consistent, reliable actions and open communication. When we build trust in our crew, they are more likely to follow instructions if you're an officer, work collaboratively, and support each other under pressure. This trust allows for seamless coordination and efficient execution of tasks, which is crucial in high-stress situations. Which is basically our job.

Leaders play a significant role in fostering trust by being transparent, honest, and dependable. Transparency is huge. Let your crew see who you are. The good and the bad. You will be exposed for who you are sooner or later. Why wait? Share your strengths and weaknesses. Get help with the weaknesses and keep growing in your strengths. I make it a point to tell my crew where I am weak and where I am strong. That way they know what I'm working on. Also, they may not be surprised when I screw something up in that area because I've been honest, Hell, they may even pick up the slack in that area if needed. Isn't that what teams do? When leaders demonstrate trustworthiness, they set a standard for the entire crew, reinforcing the importance of mutual trust. Trust also enhances morale, as firefighters who feel supported and confident in their team are more likely to be engaged.

Remember, you never automatically trust someone. Especially in the fire service. I'm not gonna lie; just because you show up and are wearing the shirt doesn't mean I trust you with my life. I've worked beside many men and women who have worn the shirt, pinned on the badge, and could not do the job. What do you think that did for our relationship? What do you think it did for building trust?

As stated, relationships take time, and in developing those relationships, trust is developed. Do not expect this to just happen right away or assume that you are trusted either. This is a job where I do believe you should have to prove yourself to your brothers and sisters. You can't build relationships without trust. How you relate to your station members as an individual is impacting your station morale.

Conflict Resolution

In any workplace, conflicts are inevitable. Especially in the fire service. I mean, we live together. We eat together and sleep together and are in each other's personal space on the regular. There is bound to be some on-shift or cross-shift conflict. However, in the fire service, where teamwork and communication are paramount, unresolved conflicts can hinder performance and negatively impact morale. Effective conflict resolution is crucial for maintaining a positive and productive work environment. Having a relationship with the people you work with makes this ten times easier. Conflict is already hard for most people. It's even harder if you don't have a relationship with the person.

Addressing conflicts promptly and constructively helps prevent misunderstandings and resentment from escalating. You should have some training in conflict-resolution techniques, such as active listening, empathy (there's that word again), and negotiation, to handle disputes effectively. Encouraging open dialogue and providing a safe space for discussing issues can also facilitate resolution. Once again, it is a lot easier if you have focused on fostering a culture of trust and relationships in your firehouse.

Conflict resolution not only helps maintain overall station harmony, but it also strengthens relationships within the crew. When conflicts are resolved respectfully, crewmembers gain a better understanding of each other's perspectives and develop stronger bonds. This improved understanding fosters a more cohesive and supportive team environment.

Respectfully is the keyword here. I have seen conflicts resolved that were not resolved. They were over for the moment because the person in charge wanted it to be, but there was no clear resolution. Without having a relationship, a situation like this can fester some pretty bad attitudes and back-alley backtalk. When resolving conflicts, make sure everyone has a chance to be heard and some follow-up is done. Conflicts in the firehouse are not always easy. Fostering a culture that is building positive relationships will make it better.

Building a Support System

A strong support system is vital in the fire service, where the demands of the job can be physically, mentally, and emotionally taxing. Building a robust support system ensures that firefighters have the resources and encouragement they need to manage the challenges they face. I could go on and on about this one. I am really big on community. You need a support system in place that you are doing life with. For some, this is friends and family, but this can extend into the fire service. Knowing you always have men and women who support you and have your back is a huge morale booster when it comes to this job.

At my first firehouse, almost twenty years ago, I was building this support system and didn't even know it. We all built real authentic relationships with each other and had each other's backs. We all had friends and family, but we were also family, and in a way, became part of each other's families. As I've gone through my career, these men I was stationed with are still some of my good friends. I consider them brothers that I can go to with anything, on or off the job. I've been through hell and back throughout my life, and these guys have always been here for me. They've been the first to show up on my doorstep on multiple occasions, and I've been the first to show up on theirs. Honestly, I wouldn't be the man or fireman I am today without these guys. You need a support system, especially when things are looking a little low.

Support systems don't have to be super personal like mine. Rhey can take various forms—church communities, mentorship programs, peer-support networks, and access to counseling services. Mentorship programs typically pair people with little life experience to people who have a lot of life experience. It works the same way in the fire service. These programs can provide guidance, support, and a sense of belonging. Peer-support networks create opportunities for firefighters to share experiences and offer emotional support to one another. Once again, not something we used to talk about, but we are getting better at it!

I believe that having access to counseling services and mental health resources is also crucial for maintaining a good support system. By providing these resources, fire departments show that they care about their members' mental health and are committed to their overall support. A well-established support system helps firefighters cope with the stresses of the job, preventing burnout and enhancing morale. At this point, I think burnout eventually comes for us all. Some of us just rename it "retirement."

Relationships in the fire service are vital for creating a positive and effective work environment and maintaining high morale. Trust ensures that crewmembers can rely on each other, which is essential for coordinated and successful operations. Effective conflict resolution maintains harmony and strengthens relationships, while a strong support system provides the necessary resources and encouragement for managing job-related stresses. By focusing on these aspects, you can build a resilient, motivated, and cohesive crew.

SECTION 4:

WAYS TO HURT MORALE IN THE FIRE SERVICE

Poor Leadership

If great leadership is good for positive morale, then poor leadership can severely damage morale in the fire service. When leaders fail to provide clear direction, support, or recognition, it undermines the confidence and motivation of their crew. Ineffective leaders might exhibit traits such as indecision, favoritism, or a lack of empathy, which can create a sense of insecurity and frustration among firefighters. This is extremely frustrating these days, with all the "leadership" talk going around.

In most departments, it does not take a lot to be in a position of leadership. There is actually nothing that requires you to be a leader at all. You take a test, score high, and get promoted. Good leadership for good morale? It's not even in the thought process. If it is, it definitely is not getting pushed through to the action phase. It's not so much that we have "bad leadership." I believe you can leave at any level. It's that we are putting people who have no business leading in leadership positions, all the while leaving the ones who would be great leaders in the dust because they're not great test-takers. Honestly, this is one I'm having trouble solving.

Right now, my only way to solve it is for you not to be one of these people. If you are in a leadership position and morale sucks in your station, it's on you, and I hope this book is encouraging you to make some changes. We have enough "leaders" not doing their job. Please do not do the same. Also, if you are not in a leadership position and morale sucks in your station, you can still lead from the jump seat. Men and women do it in the fire service every day. There is actually a book about it. It's called *Jump Seat Leadership*: *The Guide to Informal Leadership in the Fire Service*. I even know the guy who wrote it!

Hear me out. Leaders who do not engage with their crew or fail to address concerns can lead to feelings of neglect and dissatisfaction. This lack of engagement makes firefighters feel undervalued and unsupported, which can erode trust and diminish their commitment to their roles. Poor leadership not only affects individual morale but can also lead to broader issues within the team, including decreased collaboration, increased tension, and can eventually lead to isolation. That's a hard road to come back from. It can be done, but it's hard.

Lack of Communication

A lack of communication can create significant barriers to maintaining high morale. When information is not shared openly, it leads to misunderstandings, confusion, and rumors. Firefighters who feel left out of important decisions or are unaware of changes affecting their work are more likely to feel disengaged and unvalued—and a little pissed off, to be honest. Think about how many decisions have come down from the top that you knew nothing about. Not ones you didn't have a hand in making, but just knew nothing about. It makes people a little angry. I have been on scene multiple times over my career, been practicing a skill, only to be told, "Hey, man, we don't do that anymore." I mean, I'm fine with following policies, but let's make sure they are properly communicated to everyone and we don't have nine different fire departments in one department.

As you can imagine, poor communication also affects the ability of crewmembers to coordinate effectively during emergencies. Without clear and consistent communication, there is a risk of misalignment and errors, which can undermine the effectiveness of operations and increase stress levels. This lack of clarity can result in frustration and a sense of disconnection among the crew.

Toxic Environment

Anything toxic is bad. That's why it's called toxic. I mean, the word *toxic* means poisonous. A toxic environment can have a devastating impact on morale, not just in your station but in the fire service. Toxic behaviors include bullying, harassment, favoritism, and discrimination, all of which create a hostile and unwelcoming work atmosphere. Look, it happens in the fire department too. I'm not saying everyone does it or that we get it right every time. I am saying that it does happen, and we can't turn a blind eye to it. If something is going on in your house, it needs to be addressed. When firefighters are subjected to or witness toxic behavior, it diminishes their sense of safety and respect within the team. We're supposed to be working together, trusting each other, becoming a family, a brotherhood, if you'll allow me to say it.

I know, I know, there is a group of firefighters out there who say the brotherhood is dead. To that I say, okay, then what are you doing to foster a culture of brotherhood? How do you define brotherhood? For me it's simple. I touched on it earlier, actually. Brotherhood is about building a community and a support system. Toxic environments rage against everything that the "brotherhood" stands for.

A toxic environment fosters distrust and resentment, making it difficult for crewmembers to work together effectively. It can also lead to high turnover rates, as individuals seek to escape a negative work environment. The grass is not always greener, but sometimes people just need a change of scenery based on their environment. If you are in a toxic environment and ignoring the things around you, you are contributing to the morale problem you are complaining about.

Overwork and Burnout

Overwork and burnout are significant factors that can and have damaged morale in the fire service. We are consistently overworked, face long hours, respond to high-stress situations, are told we can't leave at the end of our shift, and are usually subject to inadequate rest, which can lead to physical and mental exhaustion. When the demands of the job exceed an individual's capacity to manage them, it results in burnout.

What's the definition of burnout? Burnout occurs when physical, emotional, or mental exhaustion is accompanied by decreased motivation, lowered performance, and negative attitudes toward oneself and others. It results from performing at a high level until stress and tension, especially from extreme and prolonged physical or mental exertion or an overburdening workload, take their toll. Sound familiar? Once this stage of your career is reached, it is hard to recover without some outside help, like a community, support system, peer support, or professional help. Things we have already discussed.

Burnout significantly diminishes job satisfaction and motivation, leading to decreased performance and engagement. Firefighters experiencing burnout may struggle with physical symptoms like fatigue and illness, as well as mental health issues such as anxiety and depression. The cumulative effect of overwork and burnout can lead to a sense of hopelessness and frustration, severely impacting morale.

Guys, I've been there. I've reached times in my career when I thought I was done and ready to hang it up. My personal morale was in the dumps. Thankfully for me, I've had a support system most of my career and a supportive family to help me out when needed. I've also sought professional help over the years and have learned the importance of regular days off and professional counseling on occasion. Also, not every form of counseling has been formal. It's been refreshing to talk to other men and women in the fire service who have been through the same thing and have come out healthy on the other side. This is probably where I've seen the most help.

Poor leadership, lack of communication, a toxic environment, and overwork can all significantly harm morale. Nothing you didn't know already. Addressing these issues proactively and creating preventive steps is crucial for ensuring that we feel valued, supported, and motivated. By fostering positive leadership, clear communication, a healthy work environment, and reasonable workloads, fire departments can help maintain high morale and create a more effective and resilient crew.

SECTION 5:

WAYS TO BE A POSITIVE INFLUENCE ON OTHERS

Perspective is everything. Learning to be a positive influence on others can significantly impact the morale of the men and women around you. Be someone people want to be around. How can two people work for one department and hate and love it at the same time? Easy, its perspective and the choice to see the good in your fire department and to have hope for a better future. Hope ... my favorite four-letter word. Now, while I believe in hope, hope is not a plan. So, here are a few things you can do yourself to be a positive influence and improve morale.

Lead by Example

Leading by example is one of the most effective ways to be a positive influence in the fire service. Leaders who demonstrate the behaviors, attitudes, and work ethic they expect from their crew set a powerful standard for others to follow. This principle is crucial in a high-stakes environment like ours. Here, our actions and attitudes can significantly impact both operational success and team morale.

When leaders model professionalism, dedication, and integrity, they create a culture where these values are upheld by everyone on their crew. For instance, if a leader consistently shows up on time, is physically fit, looks professional, demonstrates a strong work ethic, and handles stress with composure, it reinforces these behaviors as the norm. This can encourage crewmembers to adopt similar practices, fostering a culture of excellence and reliability.

Additionally, leading by example involves demonstrating respect and empathy. Leaders who treat their crewmembers with respect and show genuine concern for their well-being build trust and loyalty. This supportive approach helps create a positive and inclusive work environment where your firefighters feel valued and motivated. By embodying the qualities they wish to see in their team, leaders not only set expectations but also inspire and guide their crew toward higher standards.

Providing Encouragement

Providing encouragement is a fundamental way to positively influence people in the fire service. Encouragement can significantly impact a firefighter's motivation, confidence, and overall job satisfaction. Recognizing and affirming the efforts and achievements of crewmembers helps foster a supportive and motivating environment.

Encouragement can take many forms, from verbal praise and positive feedback to tangible rewards and recognition. Regularly acknowledging individual and unit accomplishments reinforces a sense of achievement and value. For example, praising a firefighter for their quick thinking during a critical situation or recognizing their consistent hard work at a team meeting boosts morale and motivates them to continue performing at their best.

Beyond formal recognition, everyday encouragement is equally important. Simple gestures, such as a pat on the back, a note of appreciation, or words of support during challenging times, contribute to a positive atmosphere. When firefighters feel appreciated and supported, they are more likely to remain engaged, committed, and enthusiastic about the job.

By consistently providing encouragement, leaders and peers help build a culture where everyone feels valued and motivated. It's not that hard to come to work every day and tell people that they did a good job when they did a good job. Don't just celebrate work accomplishments either. If someone is trying to get their real estate license, start a business, or simply looking for advice, these are areas where you have an opportunity to encourage this person. It's not always about the professional side of the fire service. Sometimes it's personal.

Promoting Inclusivity

These days, I am learning one simple truth. Everyone wants to be included and heard. People want to know they are part of the team. They are looking for identity and inclusivity. Promoting inclusivity is essential for fostering a positive work environment and enhancing morale in the fire service. An inclusive environment values and respects diverse backgrounds, perspectives, and experiences, ensuring that all crewmembers feel welcomed and valued.

Inclusivity starts with actively seeking to understand and appreciate the unique contributions of each person in your station. This includes creating opportunities for everyone to participate and share their ideas, regardless of their role or background. For example, encouraging diverse perspectives during decision-making processes can lead to more innovative solutions and a greater sense of ownership among crewmembers.

You can promote inclusivity by implementing policies and practices that support diversity and equity. This might involve ensuring fair treatment in promotions and assignments and addressing any instances of discrimination or bias promptly. Creating a culture where everyone has an equal opportunity to contribute helps build a strong, cohesive unit.

When firefighters feel they are included and respected, their job satisfaction and morale increase. An inclusive environment not only enhances individual well-being but also improves teamwork and effectiveness.

Encouraging Growth

Encouraging growth is a powerful way to positively influence morale in the fire service. Supporting the professional and personal development of firefighters helps them feel valued and invested in their careers, leading to higher motivation and satisfaction.

To encourage growth, leaders should provide opportunities for continuous learning and development. This can include offering in-house training, training programs, workshops, and seminars that help firefighters enhance their skills and knowledge. Encouraging participation in specialized courses or certifications can also provide career advancement opportunities and keep crewmembers engaged.

Mentoring and coaching are also crucial for supporting growth. Experienced firefighters can mentor newer recruits or junior firefighters, offering guidance, feedback, and support as they develop their skills. This not only helps the mentees grow but also strengthens the bonds within the team. In my department, we have development books at different levels of our career that an officer or senior firefighter will work on with junior members.

Additionally, setting clear goals and providing constructive feedback can help firefighters track their progress and stay motivated. Recognizing and celebrating achievements, whether through formal awards or informal acknowledgment, reinforces their efforts and encourages continued growth. By investing in the development of their team members, fire service leaders foster a culture of continuous improvement and ambition.

One of the biggest things I like to address with growth, certificates are not the end-all and be-all. You need to be growing beyond taking classes and sitting in front of the computer. Encourage your crew to get out and physically practice job skills. Encourage them to challenge themselves and stay physically fit. Of course, if you are not doing these things, you cannot expect that they will take your encouragement seriously. I mean, I don't take financial advice from people who are bankrupt.

Staying Positive in Adversity

This one is not easy, my friends. Staying positive in adversity is a crucial way to influence morale in the fire service. Firefighters often face challenging and high-pressure situations, on and off the job. Maintaining a positive outlook can help them navigate these difficulties more effectively. For me, this one is hard without a solid foundation to stand on. For me, my foundation is my faith. It's what helps me stay positive in moments of adversity.

It was my faith that helped me push through my military deployment safely, my faith that helped me maintain a healthy marriage, my faith that helped me when my first wife passed away, and my faith that keeps me going now. I'm not gonna say this one's easy without some sort of foundation, because it's not. All the things we talked about earlier were kind of leading to this one in a roundabout way.

You can't just "have a positive attitude." It's going to stop some of the bad things that hurt morale and start implementing some of the good things we talked about. It takes grit to develop a "don't quit" mentality, and trust me, you have it in you. If I refused to quit in the face of adversity, so can you.

A positive attitude in the face of adversity can be contagious. It inspires others around you to tackle and push through what they are going through. When you and your crew remain optimistic and focused on solutions, it helps create an environment where challenges are seen as opportunities for growth rather than insurmountable obstacles. This positive mindset encourages resilience and perseverance, which are essential for handling the stresses of our job.

Leaders can model positivity by approaching problems with a solution-oriented attitude and maintaining composure under pressure. Offering words of encouragement, celebrating small victories, and focusing on what can be controlled rather than what cannot helps maintain morale and motivation. So, remember: Focus on what can be controlled.

Additionally, fostering a supportive environment where crewmembers can share their concerns and seek help without fear of judgment contributes to a positive atmosphere. Encouraging open communication and mutual support during tough seasons ensures that firefighters feel valued and understood. This can reinforce their commitment and optimism. Two things we need if we are going to get anywhere with this morale crisis we are facing.

CONCLUSION

As we reach the end of our exploration into the fire service morale crisis, it's clear that addressing and improving morale is not just an option but a necessity for the health and effectiveness of any fire department. I've done my best to lay out a comprehensive approach to understanding and tackling this crucial issue, offering a few actionable strategies to create a supportive and high-performing crew.

We've looked at the vital role that morale plays in the fire service, emphasizing how it impacts every aspect of a firefighter's experience, from job satisfaction and performance to overall well-being. We've explored the foundations of morale, from effective leadership and communication to recognition and team building. Additionally, we've identified common pitfalls that can damage morale, such as poor leadership and overwork, and provided practical solutions for overcoming these challenges.

Improving morale is an ongoing journey that requires commitment, transparency, and active engagement from all levels of the fire service. Leaders must consistently model the behaviors they wish to see, foster open communication, and create an environment where every crewmember feels valued and supported. Recognizing and addressing issues promptly, promoting inclusivity, and encouraging personal and professional growth are essential steps in cultivating a positive work environment.

The strategies I outlined in this book are not one-size-fits-all solutions but rather starting points for tailored approaches that suit the unique needs of each fire department. It is up to each firefighter and officer to adapt these principles to their specific context, continuously assess their effectiveness, and remain dedicated to fostering a culture of high morale.

Ultimately, the goal is to break the cycle of low morale and build a resilient, motivated, and cohesive team that thrives even in the face of adversity. By prioritizing the well-being and satisfaction of every firefighter, we ensure not only their personal success but also the overall effectiveness and readiness of the fire service.

As you move forward, remember that improving morale is a dynamic process that evolves with the changing needs of your team. Embrace the challenges, celebrate the successes, and remain committed to the pursuit of a positive and supportive work environment. Together, we can break the cycle and create a fire service that stands strong, united, and prepared to meet any challenge with confidence and dedication. The future of the fire service depends on the strength and energy of its teams. With the right tools and mindset, we can achieve a more fulfilling fire service for all. I still love coming to

THE FIRE SERVICE MORALE CRISIS: BREAK THE CYCLE

work. I'm just trying to help a few others do the same. It's time to play your part, not place blame. You think we have a morale crisis? What are *you* doing to fix it?

ABOUT THE AUTHOR

I am a husband, father, fireman, author, writer, public speaker, and combat military veteran from Virginia Beach, Virginia. I have a passion for leadership, and to help men own their life regardless of circumstance. A life where you are in control of your circumstances and understand that you are called to a life of purpose.

SCAN HERE FOR MORE

Made in the USA
Columbia, SC
12 January 2025